<u>Walk the Line</u>

Walk the Line

The Art of Balance
and the Craft of
Slackline

Scott Balcom

Photos by Chris Carpenter

ASHLAND, OREGON

SlackDaddy Press
Ashland, Oregon

Printed in the United States of America

ISBN: 0-9764850-0-1

TABLE OF CONTENTS

Thank you!

To everyone who has helped to make this book possible; especially Chris Carpenter for his collaborative efforts with much of the technology and for taking most of the photography.

To Adam Grosowsky and Jeff Ellington for teaching slackline by example.

To Darrin Carter for taking highline to the next level(s).

To Chongo for keeping my story alive.

And to my wife Kate and son Adom for their love and encouragement.

WARNING

Slackline can be dangerous, resulting in injury or possibly, death. Take responsibility for your own actions, as they pertain to slackline. The hazards of slackline are too numerous to mention, and reading this book does not guarantee that danger will be avoided. This book contains only the opinions and observations of its author.

INTRODUCTION

Sʟᴀᴄᴋʟɪɴᴇ ɪꜱ ᴀɴ ᴀʀᴛ of dynamic balance. It's akin to tightrope and high wire but uses tubular nylon webbing. Rope walking of one form or another has been around for at least a couple of thousand years but has always been the realm of acrobats and daredevils. *Walk The Line* dismisses the myth that only these professionals have the skills and talent to perform such feats. This myth is perpetuated by some who walk the line in order to keep others from realizing how easy it is—which is the most important secret of walking the line. In this book are other secrets of slackline, the best type of line walking. Anyone can do it.

WHAT IS SLACKLINE?

When people see slackline they often think "tightrope."

SLACKLINE CAN BE TIGHT, but it's not rope. Slackline is tubular nylon webbing that is stretched between two points so that it is tight enough to walk on. In Slackline, no balance pole is used, and although it can be tight, the nylon always stretches, allowing it to swing and bounce.

In contrast to slackline, tightrope is usually steel cable pulled tight and guyed off to reduce vibration as much as possible. A pole is used for balance. Unlike tightrope, Slackline is usually done close to the ground.

WHY DO IT?

PEOPLE OFTEN ASK ME why I walk the line. For most people slackline is so out of context that they think of a circus. Sometimes they even ask me if I'm in the circus. When I tell them I'm not, they ask me why I do it. I slackline for many reasons: it's fun; it's good for balance, focus, and concentration; it's like ti'chi, dance, and meditation; it's both strenuous and graceful; and it feels like flying.

Doesn't everyone want to learn to fly?

People often want to know if slackline is a good cross-training activity. Slackline is a good cross-training exercise for anything that requires balance, focus, strength, grace, quick reaction time and awareness. These are attributes that would benefit anyone, but especially climbers, athletes, dancers, rowers, martial artists, surfers, skiers and snowboarders. I believe that slackline stands on it's own. Other activities and sports could be training for *it*.

I cringe at the thought of competitive slackline. Certainly, you could quantify the difficulties of certain maneuvers over others. But what's the point?

The lesson of slackline is *balance*. On the other hand, the Olympics is sorely lacking a "who can go the slowest" sport.

WHO DOES IT?

ANYONE CAN DO IT, or most anyone who possesses a normal grasp of pedestrian skill and has desire enough to learn. Children don't always fall into the second category; young adults make much better students, though I've had students in their fifties. I believe it is possible to slackline late into life.

1.
HOW TO GET STARTED

GEAR

SLACKLINE TECHNOLOGY is growing. New tools are being developed to make operations easier. Currently, it's pretty easy to get your hands on a sewn slackline, but this hasn't always been the case. I have included the best of the old school techniques, as a foundation to build from.

Traditionally slackline technology has been based on rock-climbing gear. The line is made of **tubular nylon webbing**. The size of the webbing determines the character of the line. **One-inch tubular** is a good place to start.

1" Tubular nylon webbing

WHAT YOU'LL NEED

- One Piece of continuous **1-inch tubular nylon webbing** fifty feet long
- At least four carabiners
- At least two lengths of **1-inch** tubular, 6-feet long (for runners)
- Slack shoes (optional, but recommended)

WHERE TO GET GEAR

TUBULAR WEBBING and carabiners can be bought at most places that sell rock-climbing gear. Webbing is sold by the foot and comes on a spool. When obtaining your fifty feet, be careful to watch for tape on the line, which indicates that the line has been cut. **Your line must be continuous**. At notforclimbing.com you can buy pre-sewn slacklines of varying lengths.

Carabiners come in many fancy types but a simple oval works best. Shoes with thin, smooth soles that you can feel the line with, like good skateboarding shoes work well. Cheap imitations sometimes work better, however because their soles are typically thinner, which gives you better "line feel."

2.
SETUPS AND KNOTS

WHATEVER YOU TIE your line to will need to be stronger than you think. The forces that are generated with a slackline can be great, and when setting up a line, you need to be aware of that.

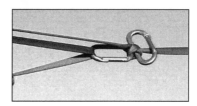

You will have a static end and a live end. The static end is fixed, and the live end is the one you tighten. This will remain the same no matter what you tie to.

Overview of Basic Setup

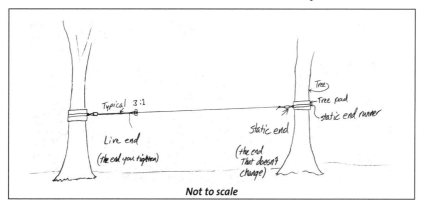

Not to scale

People who are familiar with the gear and knots may not need the detailed explanation, here's the basics.

- Lasso two trees with runners.
- Tie one end of slackline with a figure eight on a bight. Clip to first tree.
- Tie the slackline with a clove hitch six feet from second tree; clip two carabiners through clove hitch.
- Clip tail of line to second tree and back through one clove hitch carabiner; this is your 3:1.

- Pull hard on tail and tie off with a couple of half-hitches on a bight.
- Sit on the line and bounce to stretch it out, retighten and repeat until desired tension is maintained.
- Get someone to spot you and walk.

> **WARNING:** *This setup is close to the ground and should never be used up high. No one should set up a highline without first mastering low-line rigging*
> *(see Highline)*

Once you get your line, the first thing you want to do is tie a loop at the static end. This is best done as a figure eight on a bight in which the loop needs to be large enough to pass through the rest of the coiled line.

Figure 8 loop
(Figs.1-5)

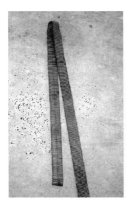  

Fig.1   *Fig. 2*   *Fig. 3*

Fig. 4   Fig. 5

I do not untie this loop; it always stays the static end.

Your first set up should be between trees; I have included trees with the other set-up possibilities in the following section.

The live end is the one you will tighten. The standard tightening technique is like a truckers knot, which gives a two-to-one mechanical advantage. Once you have clipped your static-end in place, hold the line between your fingers and walk the distance of the line. **Straighten the line as you go so the same side is always up.**

Straighten the line before tying the clove hitch.

Clove Hitch

When you pull the line tight, and the live end anchor is about six feet away, it is time to tie your clove hitch. While holding on to the point you assessed to be around six feet from your live-end anchor, take a few steps back toward the static-end, to relieve the tension you are holding. Make sure you remember which side is up while you tie your clove hitch. Figs.6-13

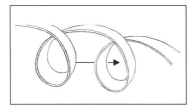

Fig. 6. Make two consecutive loops.

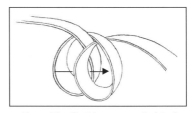

Fig. 7. The first loop goes behind second loop.

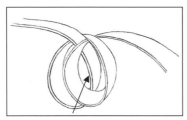

Fig. 8. Clip carabiners through both loops.

Fig. 9. It should look like this.

Fig. 10

Fig. 11

Turn the extra carabiner perpendicular to the line.

Fig. 12. If the line goes over the extra carabiner, clip through the gate.

Fig. 13. Make sure your knot looks like this.

Tie a loose clove hitch around your fingers, and clip two carabiners through the hitch. You may need to straighten the webbing, so that the knot is made with no twists. The need for two carabiners has more to do with **untying** the clove hitch after it has been tensioned than the extra mechanical advantage of using both carabiners. Before I tighten the clove hitch down on the carabiners, I turn one carabiner **in line** with the line and the other perpendicular to the line. This is the easiest position for untying the clove hitch after use. [CAUTION: **Never use the clove hitch for a highline. The clove hitch is a very weak knot and not suitable for highline use.**]

Pull on the tail of the clove hitch to cinch the line down on the carabiners. Next, clip the tail through the live-end anchor carabiner, and lead it back to the clove hitch carabiner. Make sure you do this without twisting the line. How you make these clips has a lot to do with the effectiveness of your setup. Carabiner gate orientation has to do with ease of use over safety, since your life does not depend on this sort of setup. At the clove hitch, the position of the perpendicular carabiner is not that important, it just needs to be out of the way. It *is* important that the clove hitch never tie around the gate. I prefer the anchor and clove hitch carabiner gates to be facing me, hook ends toward each other, with the tail over the clove hitch carabiner. In this position, the tail clips over the anchor carabiner, (from top to bottom) then over the clove-hitch carabiner.

Typical 3:1

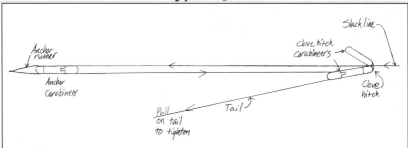

If this is done correctly, it should take an "s" shaped path, and you'll be holding the bottom of the "s," (It would make a "z" if you were on the other side of the line.) My lines are usually five to six feet off the ground. I clip down, so the tail is at the bottom, which favors a downward pull. On a beginner line that is very low to the ground, you may want your tail to end up on top, which would favor an upward pull. In this case use the top clove hitch carabiner as the active one and clip from bottom to top at the anchor carabiner and bottom to top on the clove hitch carabiner.

Figs. 14-23

Fig. 14. Pull slack out of the line.

Fig. 15. Close-up of typical three-to-one.

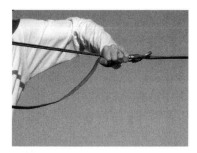

Fig. 16. Clamp down hard when line is tight.

Fig. 17. Guide long bight of tail over and through (start of first half-hitch).

Fig. 18. Adjust length of bight while tightening.

Fig. 19. Pull all slack out, and cinch on to carabiner.

Fig. 20. First tight half hitch.

Fig. 21. Second half hitch over and through.

Fig. 22. Second half hitch with slack.

Fig. 23. Second half hitch tight with enough tail.

When you pull on the tail, you will tighten the line with a three-to-one mechanical advantage (minus friction). I have seen people use a second carabiner at the live-end anchor to clip the tail through a second time and back through the second clove hitch carabiner for increased leverage. At first this seems like a good idea, but when I have tried it, it seems the extra friction overcomes the advantage of increased leverage. (This is not a perfect system because one inch tubular is one inch wide and an oval carabiner is round on the ends. However, a beginning set up does not need to be extremely tight.) While pulling on the tail, it is helpful to yank on it to break the friction that occurs in this system. Once you have the line tight, or no more yanking will make the tail end any longer, it is time to tie off the tail. The hard part is not losing any tension. Whether you are doing this by yourself or with help, the idea is to grab ahold of the line where it rounds over the last carabiner clamping down tightly and letting as little of the line as possible slip back through (fig. 16). Double the tail for about two feet (a two-foot bight), and then loop the bight over the line and carefully tie a half-hitch that takes up the slack, with this knot tight up against the clove hitch carabiner (figs. 17–19). Throw another half hitch or two and you're done. It will be important to have the half hitches on a bight when you need to untie. If you've followed all steps correctly, when untying, undo all but the initial half hitch, then pull (or yank hard if necessary) on the tail of the bight, and this knot will come undone.

A slackline stretches quite a bit, and you will never pull out all the stretch on the first tightening, especially on a new line. Initially, I get the line somewhat tight, sit in the middle, and bounce on the line while sitting. This stretches out the line. The second time, I pull a little harder and bounce a little higher. The third time, I usually pull so hard my hands hurt. Next we'll discuss what to tie the line to.

Rigging is the first challenge of slackline, and no slacker should be content to walk someone else's line. Like tuning an instrument or sharpening a chisel it is an integral part of the process, though no one sets out to learn these things.

There are lots of ways to string a line, but I will focus on three main types: trees, posts and A-frames.

3.
TREE SETUPS

IF YOU ARE TYING your line between trees, they must be strong enough to withstand a dynamic force close to one thousand pounds. Joshua trees, saguaros, and other sensitive plants should not be used. When using a tree, pad the bark in an effort to protect it against damage from the line, especially with thin-barked trees and when the direction of force is such that it cinches the line tighter.

Tree setups are easiest, because the structure is already there. The trick to tree setups is to find two trees that are the right distance apart. Both trees need to be at least eight inches in diameter, and while starting out, you will want to find two trees about thirty feet apart. It's helpful to have a tape measure or to know how long your stride is, if you wanted to pace it off. This distance does not need to be exact, twenty-five to thirty-five feet is fine, but the shorter the line, the faster and tighter the swing. A line that is too short is hard to learn on. Some people think a thirty-foot line is too short. I feel that to go too much longer is to require the line to be strung higher, which can intimidate a beginner. A thirty-foot line only needs to be two and one-half to three feet off the ground at the ends. When you step on the line, it will stretch and you will be close to the ground while in the middle. A short line does not need to be extremely tight. There is often the tendency to over tighten a short line (more on this later). Two more things to check are the ground (or landing) and the overhead, as you would with branches that would be in your way if you were up higher. Luckily, large trees often lose their lower limbs. The ideal ground would be level and covered with thick soft grass with no sprinkler heads, rocks, or other sharp or hidden objects.

You may find that perfect slack-court, but if you compromise, it is good to know the difference between luxury (grass) and danger. The most dangerous obstacles are things you could get impaled on (stakes or rods sticking out of the ground), or fall against (clothes lines or sliding glass doors in the fall zone). It's usually fine to have an obstacle at one end of the line; you could turn around before you get to it. But if the obstacle is in the middle, that can be dangerous. Once you have your spot and are satisfied with your distance, you need to pad the trees. I have two strips of carpet six inches wide and about four feet long with a loop of string on one end and a length of string on the other. I tie these pads carpet side in around the trees at the height I need for the distance to be walked. For example, if I'm setting up a beginner line at around thirty feet, I will set my ends at about two and one-half to three feet off the ground. This is very general and changes greatly as the tension of the line changes. Once your pads are in place, you will tie runners around each tree. This can be done a number of ways. The object you are tying to will determine what your runners look like. A runner could have a loop on both ends, tied with an **overhand loop** or the runner could **be** a loop, best tied with a **water knot**.

Overhand Loop
Figs. 24 - 25

Fig. 24. Bight goes under and through.

Fig. 25. Tighten.

Water Knot
Figs. 26-29

Fig. 26. Start as overhand.

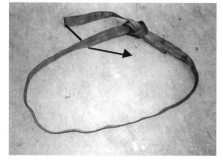

Fig. 27. Tail to tail, follow knots path in opposite direction.

Fig. 28. Guide it around and through.

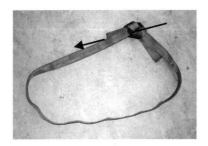

Fig. 29. Pull tight.

Runners
Figs.30-34

Fig. 30. A runner that looks like this . . .

. . .can be tied around a tree like this, or pull one end through the other creating a girth hitch. Fig. 31

Fig. 32. A runner that looks like this . . .

. . . can be tied around a tree like this (only longer). You may want to add a carbiner. Fig. 33.

It is rare to find a situation where a loop runner will be the perfect length, as in figure 31, but a second loop runner can be added if the first is too short (see fig. 34).

Fig. 34

Slacker-Hitch
Figs.35-37

For a heavy duty setup or a setup that is easy to adjust to almost any tree size, try the slacker-hitch. Use a piece of nine-sixteenths or eleven-sixteenths super tape, twenty feet long with a loop on one end. Starting at the loop end, wrap the tree with the super tape one time around, and pull the tail through the loop (see fig. 36). Making sure you have no twists in the line, lead the line back around the tree the way you came at least three times. Make sure you leave access to the loop on the lines' end. Thread a bight of the tail through the loop (see fig. 37). Tie off with three half-hitches on a bight just like the typical three-to-one (see figs. 17-23). Clip all wraps to the slackline or tightening system. No matter how much tension you put on this anchor it is always easy to untie. The slacker-hitch is also good for soft-pointing (taking all the metal out of a system). Make sure all the wraps go through the soft-point loops.

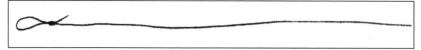

Fig. 35. Nine-sixteenths or eleven-sixteenths super tape, twenty feet long to be used as a slacker-hitch anchor.

Starting at the loop end, wrap tree with the nylon one time around and pull the tail through the loop. Fig. 36

Lead the line back around the tree in the opposite direction at least three times. Tie off to loop with half hitches. Fig.37

Always attach to all wraps of the slacker-hitch.

Trees are good temporary set ups, but I think it is unwise to leave a slackline tied to trees permanently. Trees have another disadvantage; you don't always have one where you want one.

Post Setups

If you choose to use a post, it has to be securely anchored at both the top and the bottom, such as a well-built house, carport, or porch. Fence posts are not adequate. The higher your line is on the post, the more leverage you have to pull the post out of the ground. Posts not tied at the top are more difficult to use, especially when you learn to "ride the line" and begin using the line's dynamic forces.

I started with a post set in concrete. I pulled that out of the ground. I had a post with a brace on it but pulled that out of the ground. I had a post with a brace and cables guying it, and eventually I pulled that out of the ground as well. I tried a tripod, but there were problems with that. I finally settled on the A-frame. I have found that the A-frame is far superior to any sort of post. (As it turns out, in Kazakhstan, believed to be the birthplace of circus tight-rope, they use A-frames to hold up tight-ropes).

If you had a lot of concrete, (much more than for a fence post) you could probably get a post to go the duration. I encourage A-frame usage because, contrary to popular thought, it is better than a post.

4.
A-FRAME SETUPS

A-frame construction

IF YOUR ENVIRONMENT does not provide any anchors, you will need to set up a pair of A-frames. You will need:

- Two construction grade two-by-fours or two-by-sixes, five feet long per A-frame end.
- One wooden dowel one inch or more in diameter, eight inches long per A-frame end.
- Concrete stakes, rebar, or the bottom of something secure.

If you have one existing anchor such as a tree or post, you will only need one A-frame; otherwise, you will need to build two.

Two-by-fours are usually strong enough for someone up to about 170 pounds, anyone who weighs more than that should use two-by-sixes. Regardless of weight, make sure the boards you pick are free of large knots, and make sure that they never bow too much. If A-frame boards bow or warp too much, you will need to replace them.

A-frames have the advantage that they can be set up almost anywhere. An A-frame makes a great permanent set up. (A slackline will stay soft and elastic longer if you take it down after every use, but it's nice to have a permanent set up in your yard you can walk on any time).

This particular A-frame is the product of a quest for the minimum structure necessary. Each A-frame has three components—two legs and one dowel. (Fig. 38)

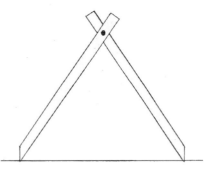

Fig. 38

With A-frames you can slackline almost anywhere.

Setting up A-frames is trickier than tying to a tree, but once you understand it, you can set up anywhere. I have used this system with success for over twelve years.

Eight feet is often the shortest length that two-by-four and two-by-sixes are sold. You only need about five feet per leg for each A-frame leg. You could buy a ten foot piece, cut in half at 55 degrees. If you cut the ten foot piece with the center of your angle intersecting the center of the board, your pieces will be the same size, or relatively close (Fig. 39).

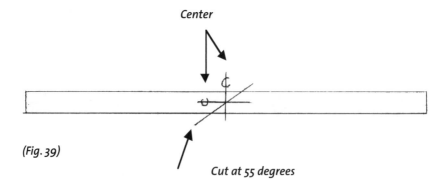

Center

(Fig. 39)

Cut at 55 degrees

Flush up the ends, measure down six inches and mark the center. This is where you will drill your dowel holes.

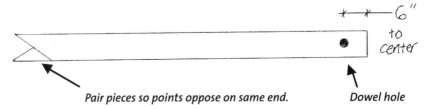

Pair pieces so points oppose on same end.   Dowel hole

Clamp and drill hole while boards are paired, staying as perpendicular to the work as possible.

While at your local lumberyard, buy a piece of hardwood dowel. Usually, you do not have a choice of wood, and dowel is most commonly sold three or four feet at a time in various diameters. A diameter of one inch will do, it is often hard to find much bigger. Get the largest dowel you can, up to one and one-quarter inch. The holes you drill need to be the same size as the dowel. If the dowel is too tight in the hole, stick the bit back in and ream it out. Cut your dowel at eight inches per A-frame.

When you are done, if you think your slackline will be too high, simply drill holes lower on the board (see drawing below).

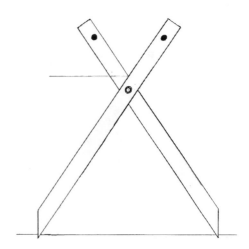

Adjustable A-frame set at
lower height

You will need to reassess the strength of the wood if you decide to use the upper holes after you've drilled lower holes. You don't want to see any knots or deflection near the lower holes.

Wood is very strong in compression strength. As long as the boards stay straight under tension, they should hold. The cut at the bottom of the A-frame leg has a "toe" and a "heel." Some people imagine the A-frame should stand on the cut, with both the toe and the heel on the ground. The A-frame will not stand this way, as there is nothing to resist the legs from spreading (see fig. 38). When the A-frame is standing on toes only, it has a chance to dig in. If you had very hard dirt or rock, or were inside, you could set a two-by-four flat on the ground, with blocks attached on the top near the ends. Only in this situation would I consider using the cuts like feet—flat footed, with the blocks at the toes like stops. This bottom completes your triangle and is called a sleeper. A sleeper is the only piece that's in tension instead of compression and does not need to be permanently attached to the A-frame. This makes a very collapsible and relatively portable A-frame for all occasions. I have been working on the next generation of slick A-frames, but I believe this is the best A-frame you could make easily yourself.

A-Frame Tie
Figs. 41-46

An A-frame tie allows you to easily clip a slackline to an A-frame and an A-frame to a descending line. An A-frame tie is a runner with a loop on both ends.

Fig. 41. Hold one loop in front of the A-frame.

Fig. 42. Guide the line over the top and around and under dowel at back.

Fig. 43. Guide it over the top.

Fig. 44. Guide it under and around front of dowel.

Fig. 45. Pull it over the top a third time.

Fig. 46. It's fine for the dowel to be too long on the descending line side.

Two short runners looped over the top of the frame will also work as an A-frame tie. Use one to clip the slackline to and the other to clip to the descending line. A slacker-hitch could also be used.

Descending Line

Fig. 47. Tilt A-frame out before tightening slackline.

Descending Line

The top of the A-frame holds the slackline off the ground, but something must hold the top of the A-frame. This supporting line descends at 45 degrees or less. If the line is any steeper than this, it will cause undue stress. If the descending line is made of nylon, it will change the character of the slackline by stretching. This stretch of the descending line allows the A-frame to move, adding movement to the slackline. I don't think this is more difficult, but it does feel different than the same length line of a different setup. (I like the extra "depth" it provides, some do not). If you don't like this extra stretch you could always use a less dynamic line, such as cable. This would be on the support line only, otherwise you wouldn't be slacklining.

A simple descending line is a long runner with a loop on one end. Clip the loop to your ground anchor. Using a carabiner, clip the descending line to the A-frame tie (see Fig. 47). Tie off the descending line using the same tie-off as the typical three-to-one (see Figs. 14–23). It is necessary to have a way to adjust the descending line. There also exists the possibility of tightening the descending line to tighten your slackline. This works best when the descending line is not very steep.

The descending line of your A-frame setup is tied to, or near, the ground. This can be done a number of ways. Sometimes posts that wouldn't be strong enough to pull on from the top are strong enough to be pulled on from the bottom, because of reduced leverage. You could tie a runner with a double girth hitch (such as a prussic knot). An expansion bolt in a concrete slab would also work.

If you had nothing but dirt or grass, you could still tie to the ground using J-stakes.

Two A-frame legs, one dowel, four J-stakes and two pairing runners.

J-Stakes (Dirt Anchors)

A J-stake is a dirt anchor you can make. J-stakes can be used when there is nothing else to tie to. If the soil is muddy or sandy, they may not hold. They work well in dry soil. The stakes I have are half-inch rebar (called number four bar). Rebar is sold in twenty foot lengths and can be bought at most lumberyards. At such a yard, they are likely to have a rebar bender/cutter that you can use to cut your bar into

Installing J-stake

(ten) two-foot pieces. (A rebar cutter is a much easier way to cut bar than a sawzall or jig saw). The same tool can be used to bend the two-foot segments into a J shape. The straight part of the J should be about eighteen inches long. If you are unfamiliar with this tool, have someone show you how to use it. Some lumberyards will cut and bend the rebar for you, usually for a price.

The J has two purposes. The first is safety, because you don't want to have sharp rebar ends sticking out of the ground. Second, the J makes the stake easier to remove. I use a sledgehammer to put Js in and a pick to take them out. The J will be upside down (see Fig. 48). No matter how far your Js are in the ground, stab the pick tip under the loop of the J and pull back. If you use the pick as a lever, the J will come right out.

J-stakes work best in pairs; if you have really hard dirt you might get away with one pair per side (they will probably bend). Two pair per side will make the setup more solid. You may even want to use three. I have found that the easiest way to rig these is to use a runner with a loop on both ends. You can use webbing (nine-sixteenths or one-inch) or small diameter rope, (five-milli-meter perlon works well and is also sold at climbing shops).

For four Js you will need two runners of two different lengths with loops on both ends. The exact length of the runners will de-pend on your situation. Start with a runner about four feet and another about six and one-half feet and make modifications if nec-essary. The length described is with the loops already tied or sewn big enough to lay the runner on the ground and set the J through it without catching the rebar on the nylon.

Fig. 48. The hook end of the J should be in-line and opposite the line of force.

Of course, you can set the Js most of the way in the ground, and then hook the loops over them, but I prefer not to. I used to pre-pair them by tying to the Js with a clove hitch, but that can be very hard to untie.

Put the first two Js in the ground equal distance from the centerline, and equal distance from the A-frames, with Js about 18" to 24" apart. The closest pair of Js should end up at least as far behind the A-frame as the A-frame is high, making an angle no steeper than 45 degrees. To measure this, simply lay the A-frame down to see how tall it is.

The second pair of Js should be farther back and out from center than the first pair. The object is to have the runner between the first pair of Js and between the second pair the same length, when pulled toward the top of the A-frame you are trying to support.

Fig. 49. Locating second pair of Js.

After setting one pair of Js, it is important to size up the position of the second pair by their runner length (see Fig. 49).

Once you have set the third J, it is important to once more assess the location of your fourth J, to insure the two runners will equalize.

Fig. 50. Checking location for fourth J.

Your runners will stretch a little, and your anchors

will shift. If an anchor shifts too much, it will pull out. The sooner the system equalizes, the stronger it will be. If a third pair of Js is necessary, you will need an even longer runner, and you'll need to repeat the positioning process. This would be the same for each end that needs an A-frame.

In rock climbing, you never want to clip a line between two anchors, because if one gives way, you won't be clipped to anything. But with dirt anchors, when you clip between a pair, you allow the anchors to shift different amounts and still be equalized. Four Js per end may not be enough in soft or sandy soil. If the Js are too close together, they will crack and weaken the earth between them and could pull out. If you try one pair and it doesn't work, it will be harder to get two pairs to work in the same spot, as you have already softened up the ground.

Fig. 51. With the slackline attached to the first anchors, check to make sure the second set will be in-line.

Once one side is set, you can set the other side. You can make sure your second set of anchors stays in line with the slackline by clipping your slackline to the first anchors and then pulling on it. By doing this, you can find your centerline and make sure your anchors will be balanced (see fig. 51). Repeat the anchor setting directions, making sure you allow room for your slackline and descending lines to have the desired lengths. Since you know how long your slackline is going to be, you could tie the clove hitch in the appropriate spot before you try to stand your whole system. Once you have anchors on both ends and ties at the top of both A-frames, you have clove hitched your slackline, and your descending lines are in place, you are ready to stand the whole show. This can be done by yourself, but it is much easier with help.

A-Frame Tips

Some tips that might help with standing an A-frame upon its own:

- Sometimes you can get an A to stand on its own, if while you hold it upright, you tap on the top ends of the A legs with your sledgehammer.
- If you have an extra J, you could dive it part way, close and low on the A-frame leg, and hook the leg in a supportive way.

Once you have your system standing, and **before** you have any real tension on it, you want to walk to the end of the line, where you can see the descending lines relationship to the slackline and the descending line on the other end. All lines should be in a straight line, with the anchors straddling your imaginary straight line. You may find your A-frames need adjustment.

When adjusting the A- frame, "walk" legs one at a time to the perfect spot. Be careful not to let the legs spread (only while the line is loose).

Before I tighten my line, I usually start with the A-frames lean-ing out away from the length of the line by about 10 degrees. When you tighten your slackline, your descending lines will also stretch, and after tightening, your A-frames are more likely to be plumb.

Make sure the points at the bottom of your A legs are oriented the same way as the A-frame drawing(see fig. 38, p.23). I usually don't have any problem with the legs spreading, but sometimes they will. A-frames work best if the distance between the legs is the same as the length of the leg to the dowel, creating an equilateral triangle.

A-frame legs should never be less than forty-five degrees to the ground. If they are, the legs will spread.

If you ever have trouble with A-frame legs spreading, simply tie a runner around the legs, below the heels. Depending on how you do this, you could set up a turnbuckle, with the addition of a stick or dowel. Twist the dowel tightly in the nylon, then turn the dowel out at 90 degrees to the twisted line. The dowel should cam against the ground and hold the desired tension, stopping leg-spread.

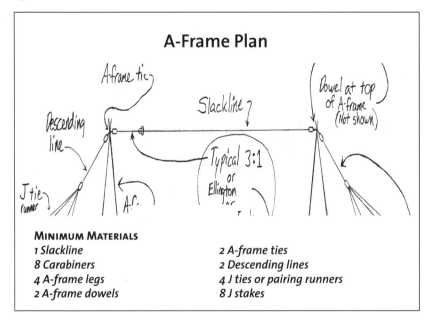

A-Frame Plan

A-frame tie

Slackline

Dowel at top of A-frame (Not shown)

Descending line

Typical 3:1 or Ellington

J tie runner

A.C.

MINIMUM MATERIALS

1 Slackline	2 A-frame ties
8 Carabiners	2 Descending lines
4 A-frame legs	4 J ties or pairing runners
2 A-frame dowels	8 J stakes

J-Stake Removal

In very sandy soil, you may want to use a sand anchor instead of a dirt anchor. If you have success with your J-stakes and then it rains and the ground gets muddy, you could easily pull your anchors out if you walked on the line before the ground dries. If it rains and you don't walk your line until the ground dries, your anchors should be fine.

Stab pick under J, lever out of the ground.

After the initial levering, use the tip of the pick to tap the J up.

Car Anchors

Cars and trucks make for fast, but poor, anchors for a slackline setup. I've never liked the spongy, out-of-rhythm bouncing you experience when using them. While using an A-frame, you can eliminate the bouncing and still use your car as an anchor.

Lay a long runner with a loop on both ends on the ground in a V shape. The open end of the V should be as wide as your wheelbase. Drive over the knots, and put small stones in the loops, behind the tires. Back up to where the loops with the stones in them are tight against the back of the tires, and the runner is under both tires. Your descending line clips to the runner. The rest of the setup will be the typical A-frame already discussed.

In a parking lot or a place with very hard dirt, the points on the bottom of an A-frame don't always work well. At the very least, the legs need to be tied together at the bottom to keep from spreading. What works even better is to have a piece of wood at the bottom, to complete the triangle. A flat two-by-four lying on the ground with blocks attached to stop the A-frame legs from spreading works well.

5.
Other Tightening Systems

SOME PEOPLE CALL the basic three-to-one tightening system "the primitive system," and in a way they're right. Getting your first half-hitch tight is the crux move and requires strength, dexterity, and practice to perfect.

If you follow the directions and don't try to get the line tight on the first pull, you will be more successful. While using the basic three-to-one with a tree setup, if your tail is long enough, you can increase leverage by wrapping the line around your hand, stepping behind the tree, then quickly stepping your feet on the back of the tree and leaning back, using your legs and bodyweight to gain the extra leverage. Here again, the tie-off will be the hard part. You can either hand-over-hand your way back to the clove hitch, holding the tension as you go, or have a friend at the clove hitch hold the tension. You can also continue your way around the back of the tree, using the tree as a brake. Clearly these ways are primitive and take a lot of effort.

While you're learning to tighten the line, pay attention to the tightness you prefer. Don't fall victim to the "if only I could get it tight enough, I could walk it" syndrome. I've seen people use this as an excuse if they can't get over the squirrellyness of the line.

Remember, short lines don't need to be extremely tight. On the other hand, if you like the tight line style, you'll never get your line tight enough with the "primitive method."

The next thing to consider is that at the clove hitch, you can change the type of line you are using. After tying the clove hitch and clipping the carabiners through the hitch, pull hard on the tail to set the knot. Now, you can clip anything you want to the clove hitch carabiner.

Come-along

A come-along has lots of pulling power, but also serious drawbacks. A come-along weighs a lot, and this extra weight on the line can be felt as feedback, which is a distracting and unwanted influence on the line, created as the weight that causes it tries to catch up to where the line has already been.

To remedy this problem, I once had a post set up with a pulley at the top and a come-along tied to the bottom. The cable of the come-along went up, parallel to the post, and turned at a right angle as it went through the pulley. At the end of the cable was a hook that the slackline was tied to, with a clove hitch a few feet away from the post. The right angle greatly reduced the amount of power available to tighten the line, although yard constraints made a lesser angle impossible. The real drawback to this system, however, is the way the cable under tension twists the slackline. As you will see, it is most comfortable to walk a line that has no twists.

Ratchets

A ratchet is similar to a come-along but tightens strap rather than a cable. I own many of these tools but I never use them for tightening a slackline. Although some people repackage these tools as slackline tools, in my experience they are too heavy, don't have enough scope and don't work as easily as the Ellington.

Rock-climbing gear

Some people change over to rock-climbing rope at the clove hitch and use tools made for rope handling, such as pulleys, brakes, and belay devices. One system I have used employs a rock-climbing pulley at the live-end anchor and a Grigri belay device at the clove hitch, or vice versa. The Grigri locks off automatically after the pull, making the tie-off just a back up. The Grigri also has a cam-release lever that makes it easy to let the tension off the system.

Some pulleys have a rope-locking cam attached that would also lock off on the rope, but most of these lack a release lever. When it comes time to undo this setup, you can either pull extremely hard on the tightening system to undo the cam, or simply clip the static end to your rock-rope tightening system. You could then set up your line with a short, typical, two-to-one on the other end. If this is done correctly, you can take your initial pulls from the two-to-one and then pull on the rope tightening system with no problem. The two-to-one tie-off, when done correctly, will come undone no matter how much tension is on it. In this way, you could have a cam locked down on your tightening rope but still untie your two-to-one. This system works best for a long line between trees. On a long line, you need more "scope," which is the available length of tightening. To increase the scope, move the clove hitch further from your anchor.

If you don't already have some of these rock-climbing tools, don't worry about it because this method, unless you add more pulleys, is not as good as the Ellington. I also know people who have broken Grigris in this way.

The Ellington
Figs.52-58

After I'd been walking slackline for some years, Jeff Ellington showed me the method he uses to tighten his line. This method does not work well with one-inch tubular, but you could use a piece of nine-sixteenths tubular to tighten a one-inch slackline. The Ellington is a self-locking six-to-one, minus the friction.

If you are walking nine-sixteenths tubular or smaller, you could use the line you're walking as the tightening system.

To tighten a one-inch slackline with nine-sixteenths, tie a clove hitch on your one-inch line and clip two carabiners through the hitch as you normally would, except instead of making one carabiner perpendicular, make them lineup, (see fig.53). **Pull hard on the tail of the slackline to set the clove hitch firmly on the carabiners.**

Get a piece of nine–sixteenths about thirty feet long; tie a loop on both ends.

How you proceed from here depends on whether you will pull up or down, from the right or left. In the picture sequence, my line is high enough to pull down, but I will demonstrate the clip sequence for the upward pull. Clip one end of the tightening line to the top clove hitch carabiner. Everything else is set up like the basic two-to-one with the gates of both the live-end anchor and lower clove hitch carabiners facing you, with the hook ends toward each other.

Fig. 52. Clip loop to top clove hitch carabiner; clip anchor carabiner, top to bottom.

Fig. 53. Clip bottom clove hitch carabiner bottom to top.

Fig. 54. Keeping the line flat, clip around these two points in a circular direction a total of three times.

Fig. 55. The end of the second loop will look like this.

43

Fig. 56. Clip anchor carabiner for third time.

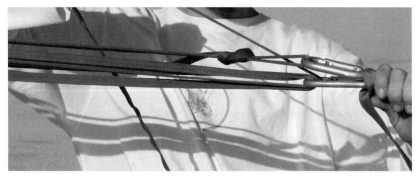

Fig. 57. Make three full circles, ready to pull.

Fig. 58. As I pull down on my setup to favor an upward pull, the line twists, increasing friction and greatly reducing efficiency. The first clip sets you up for an upward or downward pull.

To favor an upward pull

The tightening line travels from the clove hitch to the anchor and clips from **top to bottom**. It continues to the lower clove hitch carabiner to clip from **bottom to top**. In this way you are making a **loop** instead of an S. Continue around the loop two more times, and then tighten by simply pulling on the tail. As you do this, the loop on the outside moves to the inside, creating a friction knot that locks off when you let go.

Depending on how much "scope" you were shooting for when you tied your clove hitch, you may or may not have enough tightening line to make three complete loops. If you fall short, you should be able to pull in the direction of your next clip, which should be the last clip, and pull out enough slack to make your last clip. If you end up with too much left over before you start to pull, you don't have enough scope.

I usually back up the lock off with a half hitch or two on a bight; but the times I have not backed it up, it has held.

To favor a downward pull; this is mostly the same as an upward pull but the first clip at the anchor carabiner is from bottom to top, and the second clip at the lower clove hitch carabiner is from top to bottom. Follow this loop around three times.

How to untie the Ellington
Figs.59-61

Fig. 59. Unclip the last clip.

Fig. 60.

Fig. 61. Yank hard.

To untie the friction knot, unclip your last clip and yank hard. It may take more than one pull. The first unclip is the hardest. Work backward, unclipping opposite of how you originally clipped. After about the third unclip, the tension will overcome the friction, and the knot will come undone. If the tension on the line is so great that the first carabiners gate is locked, sit on the line and bounce out some of the tension. Quickly untie the line, as there is a time/rebound factor. Or thread the tail back through the carabiners the way it came, pulling the line out with a yank as you go.

This method is not commonly used but should be. The Ellington has the highest power to cheapness ratio of any thing I know of.

In case you're wondering, one inch tubular will wrinkle as it goes around the inside curve of an oval carabiner. If you clip three times around with one inch, your line will get bogged down with friction.

It is good to dedicate a line as an Ellington line, as the process of tightening can ripple and even burn the line.

Slack-Jack™

The Slack-Jack™ is a brand slackline adjustment tool that I am in the process of patenting. The Slack-Jack™ is an improvement over the Ellington, it has less friction to overcome and is easier to use and release.

The Slack-Jack™ uses a heavy-duty, three-quarter-inch nylon webbing line that weaves between two components fitted with pulley-rollers for a six-to-one mechanical advantage. The easy release self-locking brake is a leverage brake, which is a unique feature of the Slack-Jack™.

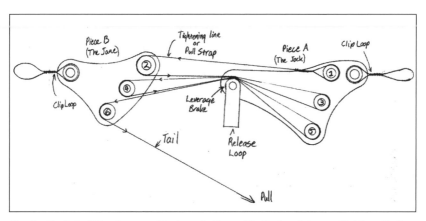

Fig. 62. Slack-Jack™ cut-away. Clip loop bolts and bolt at point 1 are tight on their spacers. Points 2 through 6 and leverage brake have rollers that need to roll freely.

Piece A is called the Jack and piece B is called the Jane. The tightening line starts at point 1 on the Jack and goes over and under point 2 on the Jane, over and under point 3 on the Jack and so on, (see fig. 62). All line segments travel **over** the leverage brake. The clip loops attach to the anchor and slackline.

The diagram shows pieces A and B close together (appropriate while not in use). In this position, the tail will be very long. To use the Slack-Jack™, you must first add line to the system. Attach the Jane's clip loop to anything, or have a friend hang on to it while you tip the nose (where the leverage brake is) of the Jack down. Pull with one hand, while making sure the tail feeds in straight (**with no twists**) with the other. Tip the Jack back and forth to find where the line feeds the easiest. The more the line feeds out, the greater the scope of tightening. If you pull the end of the tail past point 6, the Slack-Jack™ will still work, only not as well, but **the tail cannot go past the leverage brake and still work.**

Once you feed all the line into the system, and before you have tension on the slackline, you need to take care not to tangle the lines of the Slack-Jack™. Making sure there are no twists in your slackline and no twists in your Slack-Jack™, attach the Jane's clip loop to the slackline and the Jack's clip loop to the anchor. As you pull on the tail, allow time for slow loops of slack to get sucked up by the system (only an issue under low tension). The Jack and the Jane should always be in line with each other. As you pull on the tail, watch to make sure the Jane does not twist in relation to the Jack. This is controlled by the direction of pull. Try to pull inline with the slackline, or close to it.

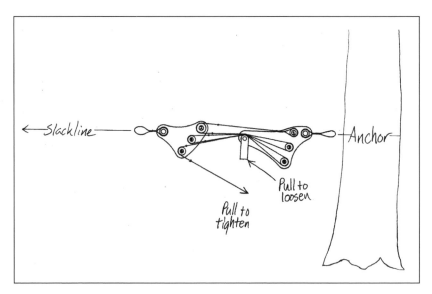

Fig. 63.

Just like the other ways of tightening the line, when you have a lot of tension, you need to pull with a yank, to break the friction. If you are just walking, you may not have to back up the Slack-Jack™ brake. But if you are doing jumping tricks, you may want to tie a couple half hitches up close to the Jane, where the tail comes out, or remove the Slack-Jack™ from the system after tightening.

When it comes time to break down, clip a carabiner on to the release loop, hold on to the tail to regulate release rate, and pull on the carabiner, which will release the brake.

Many release strategies are based on an all or nothing mentality. With the Slack-Jack™ you have the ability and control to let off a little tension. This is useful if you like a different tension than one of your fellow slack'ers. As you take turns, you can easily change tension to suit.

Once you have released all the tension on the Slack-Jack™ and have unclipped the Jane from the line, you must once more be careful to keep the lines from tangling. Hold the clip loop of the Jane while you pull on the tail. Pull on the clip loop to pull out slack loops in the system. Go back and forth between these two, until the Jack and Jane are close together again. Now wrap the tail around the lines between the Jack and Jane several times, then daisy chain the remaining tail.

To tie a daisy chain, start an overhand knot, but don't pull the tail all the way through. Once you have a loop through the start of a knot, pull another loop through the first loop, and another loop through the second loop, and so on, until you have a whole string of loops. When you have less than a foot left over, pull the tail through the last loop; this should keep the loops from coming unraveled.

To untie the daisy chain, take the tail out of the last loop and pull. All the loops should come undone.

Slack-Dog™

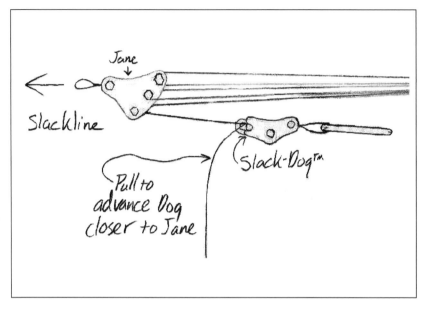

Fig. 64

As I developed the Slack-Jack™, I thought of other tools that would be useful. One is the Slack-Dog™ line handler. When using rope to tighten a line, some people use an ascender to grab on to the rope. (An ascender clamps down on the rope to make it easier to pull.) The Slack-Dog™ does this for webbing. The Slack-Dog™ is a very simple and useful slackline tool. While using a Slack-Jack™, the dog attaches to the tail as a handle. Pull on the Dog to tighten the Slack-Jack™, The Slack-Dog™ will not slip in the pull position, and more tail will pull through the Slack-Jack™. If you pull on the tail after it goes through the dog, it will cinch up on the Slack-Jack's tail for the next pull.

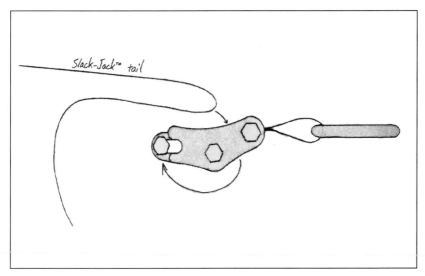

Fig. 65

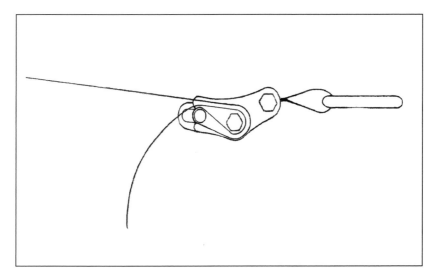

Fig. 66

Threading the Slack-Dog™

Fold the Slack-Jack™ tail under itself creating a "bight." Feed the bight through the Dog between the clip-loop bolt and the center bolt on the same side as the single inside curve. Pull enough bight through the Dog that you can easily wrap the bight around the center bolt and feed the loose bolt through the end of the bight (see fig. 65). Pull out the slack, making sure the loose bolt sets in its notch and the line you are attaching to is cleanly in place (see fig. 66). If this is done correctly, you will be able to pull on the Dog and it will not slip on the Slack-Jack™ tail (it is useful to have a carabiner clipped to the Slack-Dog™ as a handle). If you pull on the tail after it comes out of the Dog, it will synch up closer to the Slack-Jack™. The outermost line is the line that will lock off and the inner line is the one that can advance. A one-inch Slack-Dog™ can be used to adjust the length of the slackline instead of using a clove hitch.

Multiplier

With the help of a Slack-Dog™ and a dog-tail it is possible to multiply the Slack-Jack's six-to-one mechanical advantage to a twelve-to-one or even a twenty-four-to-one. It is helpful but not manda-

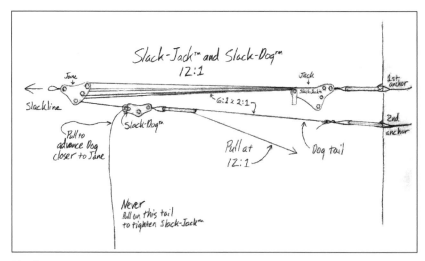

Fig. 67

tory to have a second anchor below the Slack-Jack™ anchor to attach the dog-tail to. A dog-tail is a piece of nine-sixteenths tubular nylon webbing, ten to twenty feet long, with a loop on one end.

For a twelve-to-one, a ten-foot line will do. Attach the dog-tail to the second anchor and run the tail through the carabiner attached to the clip-loop of the Slack-Dog™. This will create a two-to-one that does not add to but multiplies the Slack-Jack's six-to-one (see fig. 67).

To turn the twelve-to-one into a twenty-four-to-one, add a second carabiner at the second anchor, and clip through in a circular path. Next, run the dog-tail back to the Slack-Dog™ carabiner and clip through continuing in a circular path, similar to the Ellington. Pull with a twenty-four-to-one mechanical advantage in the same direction as shown in the twelve-to-one.

6.
LINES

Now everyone understands that it's line and not rope, right?

- <u>Nylon Rope</u>. This is terrible stuff to walk on. It can roll off your feet and whip you in the hand, arm, and crotch. You must pay very close attention to make sure the rope does not roll past your big and little toes. This is not conducive to swinging the line.

- <u>Other ropes.</u> Thick ropes don't roll as much, but they don't stretch either. Polypropylene rope is boring compared to slackline.

- <u>One-inch flat nylon.</u> This is most commonly used for backpack strap, and works great for that purpose. As a slackline, it is a disappointment. It stretches a lot at first, and then is sort of dull and limp. It has sharp edges that are more likely to cut you as you pop off the line. Worst of all, it is very difficult to untie.

- <u>One-inch tubular nylon.</u> This is the standard slackline. It's a good beginner to intermediate line. It is mildly dynamic and somewhat predictable. As one-inch gets longer, it starts to get harder, especially if it's loose. A long line on one-inch is for more advanced slackliners, as it becomes less predictable.

- <u>Two-inch tubular nylon.</u> Slower and duller than one-inch, two-inch tubular doesn't have much bounce. You must stand over the center of the line. If you had a way of tightening that could keep the line flat, it would add to the stability, but as soon as you tie a knot, the line can twist.

- <u>Nine-sixteenths-inch tubular nylon.</u> This is sometimes called "super tape." I call it racing line. This is a fast and dynamic line for advanced walkers. It can mercilessly punish the unskilled but also richly reward those who flirt long enough to find her fruits.

- Half-inch tubular nylon. This line is what big-wall climbers make hero loops out of. Half-inch is a lightweight line that's not suitable for long lines. It can be fast and could leave welts.

- Bootlace. This is tubular nylon shoelace. It is sold on a spool so you could buy a long enough piece to walk on if you can get it tight enough. It is not quite strong enough to use as a slackline (my piece broke shortly after I got it tight enough).

- Threaded lines. These are lines made up of more than one piece of nylon. When I walked the Lost Arrow Spire, I threaded two pieces of nine-sixteenths inside a piece of one inch. All lines were full length with no brakes. This made a strong line, although it was heavy and subject to feedback (see Highline, pages 107-109). Built-ups are harder to tighten because they weigh more and aren't very effective at doing the typical two-to-one (see other tightening systems). The triple line is strong and heavy and not that fun to walk close to the ground unless you're practicing for a highline. A double line with one nine-sixteenths inside a piece of one inch is more fun to walk close to the ground, but less safe up high. Doublers make good long lines, they have lots of depth. I have a line-threading needle that is made from a single piece of thick copper wire. I hammered one end flat and drilled a couple holes in it, (to tie the inner lines with a thin wire) then bent the 30" needle at greater than a right angle. After threading lines it is important to pull hard on the outside line to stretch it. If this is not done, as you tighten that slackline the inner lines will come tight first and rattle inside the line, like a rattle snake.

Photo by Kate Balcom, 1985

Fig. 68. Scott Balcom walking slack cable, Marin Peninsula.

- <u>Chain and cable</u>. Sometimes you can find cable strung through lines of short posts. If the end posts are properly anchored and the cable's the right tension, it can be fun to walk on these cables. When you step on the cable, all the slack comes to the span where you stand. The spans are usually short, and if you need a break, you could stop to rest on top of a post. The cable may be up to two hundred feet long. If you step over the post, all the slack slides from where you've been to where you're going, which can be fun and challenging.

- <u>Wire</u>. I once saw a guy with a very small cable he called wire. In fact, it was just like the small cable used for wired stoppers for rock climbing. Slackline seems to prepare you better for non-dynamic walking than chain, cable or wire prepares you for slackline; he couldn't walk my slackline, but I could easily walk his wire.

7.
CENTERING

FOCUSING ON BALANCE is not about mental effort. Balance is a state of being, not thinking. You feel it in your body, not your brain. Like martial arts that train you to center your energy at your physical center (one and one-half inches below your naval), slackline can also teach this principal.

In Western thought, we tend to live in our brains, so most people try to think their way through problems. In slackline, your goal should be to center your energy from **low in your body**. From this perspective of being centered low in your body, you are much closer to the line, which makes it much easier to balance.

Before you step on the line, it is good to center. If you jump up on the line and *then* try to balance, you will almost certainly fall. If you get centered in balance **before** standing on the line, you have much more control. There are many ways to do this, but mainly you just want to stop, take a couple of deep breaths, clear your mind, and focus **from** center.

It is important to be relaxed. **If you relaxed completely, you would fall off.**

Try to relax *almost* completely.

8.
LESSONS & LINE POSTURES

Slackline fact number one: you will fall off.

Slackline fact number two: You can fall from a slackline in a split second, and the results could be serious injury or worse. Take whatever precautions you feel are necessary to insure your safety.

Any rules or guidelines set forth here are meant to minimize bad style and speed up the learning process. New slackline styles are always evolving. These new styles may require a different approach or technique.

If you break the rules well enough, new art will be made.

Once you feel that the line is tight enough, sit on it in the middle, bounce up and down, and swing back and forth. This stretches the line. You might find that you need to re-tighten, and you may even need to move the clove hitch further out on the line (re-rig). New lines will stretch quite a bit, so it may take some time to get it right. When you think your line is tight enough, it is still a good idea to bounce and swing **while sitting**. This tells you the parameters of the line, how far it will swing, and how much it will bounce. The only difference between sitting and standing is your center of gravity.

In the beginning, it is best to have a spotter. Don't expect your first time on the line to be graceful; just lean on your spotter and get the line under your feet.

Foot Position: Aligned With The Line

Some people, especially those who are into board sports, may have the urge to stand sideways on the line, or off square to it. This may seem more stable at first, but this is a bad habit and will cause problems. In board sports, a sideways stance is necessary to leverage a board in a turn. On a slackline, leverage is eliminated. Even with a wide line, the center of the line is the balance point. It is best to feel the line right through the ball of your foot with your big toe on one side and the rest of your toes on the other side. Your heel should be centered. It is important to develop the *aligned with the line* awareness: your feet should be aligned with the line.

When you have both feet straight on the line, put one hand in the air and the other on your spotter's shoulder, arm, or hand. A lot of people might want to go for it from here, but you should take a little time to once more check the parameters of the line by bouncing and swinging while you're standing on it. Check out the centering effect of the bounce, but keep in mind that if you come down a little wrong, it can send you off the line. The line will bounce and swing, which is the dynamic force of it in action. Once you have an idea what to expect from the line, go ahead and start to walk, keeping your spotter near.

Don't Look at Your Feet

There is a strong tendency to look at your feet and to use your eyes to tell you where to step next. The line may be moving quickly, making it hard to judge, but remember that you already have a foot on the line. You know where that foot is, so without looking, put your stepping foot directly in front of your standing foot. Keep your legs close together while you step. The line can move quickly, so be careful.

Keep Your Eyes Focused

It is very useful to choose a focal point. This keeps you from looking at your feet; helps for concentration, and you may be surprised at how much balance is based on visual cues.

The Language of Correction

Chances are, a slackline is different than anything you have ever walked on before. Most things you could walk on (balance on) are solid or have a very tight vibration. In such a situation, you need to balance your body over that point. While slacklining, you want your body to stay over that point, while you allow your feet to swing with the line.

As a beginner, you should have someone spot you. Some people refuse a spot or let go of their spotter right away. In most cases it is useful to have someone or even two people spot you while you walk, bounce, and swing the line. This is true for at least the first couple of minutes on your first attempt and at the start of each session while you are a beginner. It is not a sign of weakness to have someone spot you. Developing a feel for the line is critical. I have seen people who use a spotter progress faster than people who want to let go right away. On the other hand, if you don't eventually let go of your spotter you will never learn, or if you lean too much on your spotter, you are not learning to feel the line.

With slackline, the first thing to learn is to be subtle enough to stay on the line; you cannot force it or muscle it. Success with slackline requires finesse. Standing or walking on the line is a lot like driving down a straight road. No matter how straight the road, you can't stop steering. You must anticipate which side of the road your car wants to veer toward and make small adjustments to compensate.

Don't try to run across the line or see how many steps you can make before you fall. You need only to be concerned with learning what it *feels* like to make a correction. If you start to loose your balance, don't start flailing your arms about. Just move your hands slowly away from the direction you're falling.

While driving, you would never keep your arms tense and straight, choking the wheel. The same principles apply to slackline. When you have mastered the line, simply walking is as mindless as driving down a straight road.

With elbows bent and hands relaxed you have the opportunity to effect balance by moving one hand closer and one hand further away. The "language" of correction is spoken in movement. You must learn to listen to balance. Each movement begins and ends in balance. There is no need to "reach out" to find balance—it is *in* you.

Arm Position

The posture in the picture to the left might run contrary to your concept of balance. Some people think of tightrope walkers with long poles, and they think their arms need to be as extended as possible. A balance pole does make it much easier to balance. But if you watch carefully tight-rope walkers hold the pole with their nearly straight arms at their sides and move the pole to the side that needs more weight. You will rarely see someone with a pole moving it up and down.

Knees and Hips

It is important to start with the proper posture, and knee and hip position is very important. Knees should be bent just enough to be over the balls of the feet with the hips centered between the feet (Fig. 69). If you are on one foot, your hips should be centered above the foot. Your shoulders should be centered over your hips, especially when turning, which we'll discuss later.

Fig. 69

For beginners, the precariousness of the line, the way it bounces and swings, can be difficult. If you can absorb some of this wildness with your knees, your hips should stay on center. This means that your arms only need to keep your head and shoulders over your hips. If you can steer with your knees your upper body will remain still.

When you steer with your knees, most of the momentum is below the knee (Fig. 70). The line will swing a little back and forth, and you should avoid waving your arms. If you're swinging your arms, you are too stiff. Your legs should be taut but relaxed.

If your hips start to get out of line, point your knees toward the direction that needs more weight, which will bring your hips in line.

If you get on the line and it swings wildly back and forth, get off the line, stop its movement with your hand, and look at the

Fig. 70

Figs. 71-72. Holding knees together can help you stabilize shaky legs even when stepping.

line: it doesn't shake at all when there's nothing to influence it. When you get back on the line, make sure your feet and legs are as relaxed as possible. Remember, the line doesn't shake; you shake the line.

You will need to develop a certain amount of strength. Keeping your knees together, even while walking is a good way to start building that strength without shaking the line.

Don't worry if you swing the line. You don't want the line to shake, but it's fine if it swings. It is important to be patient and let the line swing in its natural rhythm. The lines rhythm has to do with the type of line you are walking, as well as how long and tight it is. Since the line is tied at each end, it will swing most in the middle.

Ground Mount

While mounting the line from the ground, start around one-third the way down the line, facing toward the other two-thirds. You will do this for two reasons: First, the center and the ends are the extremes of the line, so this is a comfortable average. Second, if your line is close to level, the angle of the line behind you (one-third) is greater than the angle of the line in front of you (two-thirds). It is easier to start facing the lesser angle, especially from a sitting position (Fig. 73).

Fig. 73

There's a centering ritual that I often perform before standing up on the line. With one foot on the line and one foot on the ground, I raise my arms, inhale, and imagine the center of my body. I exhale as I lower my arms, and then as I inhale for the second time, I raise my arms and stand up on the line. As I ascend to the line, all my mental and physical momentum is going up with me. As my weight comes down on the line, I exhale and softly bring down my mental focus and energy into my body.

The particulars of how you mount the line are unimportant. It is important that you understand that stepping up onto a slackline is not like stepping up onto something solid, in which case you would push down with the leg of your upper foot. On slackline, this is not a good idea, as your foot will have the tendency to shake radically back and forth. When stepping onto a slackline, you first want to know the zero point of the line. Put one foot on the line and let it swing a little back and forth. The center of the swing is the balance point, or zero point. If you scoot or hop your other foot (the foot on the ground) over so your leg is just barely touching the line, you can stabilize the line with your leg. From this position, it is possible to jump straight up (pushing **off** with the foot on the ground) and come straight down (**on** the foot on the line), as opposed to an up-and-over mount, which could cause the line to swing. When some people mount the line, they keep their arms, energy, and focus "up". They are stuck in their brains as they try to *think* of balance.

It is beneficial to bring your focus down to center as your weight starts to bear down on the line.

There is a feeling you get when you are centered, or balanced, on the line. Pay attention to it. The object is to feel it all the time.

Standing On One Foot

People often think that they need to get their second foot on the line as quickly as possible, because standing on one foot must be harder. This is not true. Standing on one foot is generally easier. Most people will find they have a strong foot and a weak foot.

Standing on the weak foot may feel precarious. At first, try James Brown's approach and "get on the good foot." While standing on one foot, you'll have the opportunity to use the other foot for balance, like a paddle in the water. Practice this with a spotter until you feel like you don't need one. It is important to get comfortable on one foot. When you are comfortable standing on either your right or left foot, walking will be much easier. Following through with this exercise will make you a much better slackline walker in the end. One of the most common problems I see with beginners is when they are stepping quickly to avoid being on one foot. When that anxious stepping foot hits the line, it typically strikes the line from the side, causing it to swing. Beginners seem to associate the swing with the fact that they were on one foot, not that they kicked the line and made it swing. **While walking or mounting, your stepping foot should meet the line as softly as possible**.

The standing foot needs to retain all of your weight until the stepping foot is securely on the line. This way of walking is different than regular ground walking where, to quote Lori Anderson "is like walking and falling at the same time." While on a slackline, you never want to get to that, "and then catching yourself from falling" point. In this way you're always on one foot. You will need to develop your weak foot.

Taking Steps

Once you start taking measured, controlled steps, you're getting the hang of it. At some point, you will probably get mentally or physically tired, or swing the line too much. Keep up the good work. If you're not taking steps, reread this section. Some things might make more sense as you become more experienced.

Fig. 74. Keep all weight on the standing foot .

Fig. 75. Move weight on to the stepping foot only after it feels secure.

Turning

Once you start taking more than a few steps, you will quickly realize that you'll need to learn how to turn. Once you do, you will be free to roam the length of the line. Most people imagine slackline is an action sport, so they lean forward. A forward stance is great for skiing, but not for slackline. Slackline requires a much more upright approach; the center of your head should be above the center of your shoulders. The center of your shoulders should be above the center of your hips, and your hips should be centered over your feet. If your head is too far forward when you try to turn, you will have a very unstable feeling. Slackline taught me about the importance of posture. By listening to balance, I learned that having my head over my feet made my turns much more solid.

Visualization for Turning

This is what I visualize to help me keep my balance, perhaps it will help you. I imagine I can feel exactly which way gravity is pulling me, and I imagine a plumb bob is strung from over my head, its line going through the center of my head, shoulders, hips, and foot. The bottom of the plumb bob is usually in the dirt, sometimes well below the actual ground surface.

This visualization promotes a cylindrical point of view; I have the plumb line as center and my hands create a radius from center. As I walk in this plumb cylinder then go to turn, I imagine that I'm rotating in the plumb cylinder. The center point has not changed, and my focus of energy is extended below the line. This is a very powerful visualization and a somewhat advanced technique, but turning is the hardest thing everyone must learn, and it seems to help tremendously with that. To never learn to turn is to be a perpetual beginner; to never master the turn is to never move beyond intermediate. I believe that learning this technique, will help you to master the turn in a fraction of the time it would take to learn through trial and error. I cannot stress the importance of visualization enough, (see "Visualization," pp. 92-94).

The Three Movements of Turning
Figs.76-78

Fig. 76. 1. Step one foot square to the line.

Fig. 77. 2. Stand on it, turn other foot around.

Fig. 78. 3. Now walk the other way.

To view balance three dimensionally is to understand front-side back-side, right-side left-side, and up-down movement. The biggest problem with this way of seeing is backside. Backside is the blind spot, the place you cannot see. Our society places great importance on vision, but seeing is not *being*. To think of yourself in a plumb center with a radius around you is to promote **back-side awareness**. To be aware of what is behind you is to not fear it.

You'll want to turn before you get too close to the end of the line. It is difficult to turn at the very end. The closer you get to the end of the line, the tighter the vibration gets. When you find a comfortable turning spot, turn your stepping foot perpendicular to the line. Now stand on the arch of that foot, while turning your other foot around (see Fig. 77). Now you are ready to walk back the way you came. This sounds easy, and when done right, it can be.

I no longer turn this way because I have developed what I call a slur turn. When I'm ready to turn, I set my stepping foot down on the line, cocked so the line runs diagonally across my arch from near my little toe to the inside edge of my heel. From this position, I pivot on the arches of both feet at the same time, which puts me in a position similar to how I started. I can then walk the other way.

9.
BEYOND THE BASICS

Once you have a grip on the basics, it's time to branch out. The next step could be a longer one-inch line, forty to forty-five feet. If you've started on a twenty to thirty foot line as recommended, you'll know it's time for a change when you get bored. Slackline is exciting at every level. There are many lines and styles to try. Some people walk really tight, short lines no more than two feet off the ground, a style that favors jumping tricks, where the walker's feet leave the line. Some walk really long lines. Others walk skinny lines like nine-sixteenths. Some walk threaded lines. Add in different tensions and different lengths, and there are many style possibilities. New tricks are invented every day, so I won't attempt to catalog them here.

Other Slackline Skills

STANCES. There are three main ways to orient your feet on the line: The "aligned" way talked about earlier, the board sport stance, and the perpendicular stance.

PERPENDICULAR. This stance requires you to commit to front-side back-side orientation. Your shoulders should be in-line with the line, your hands the same height in front of you. Balance is quite a bit different this way. Both hands move together, in and out or up and down (Fig. 79-80).

Fig. 79

Fig. 80

BOARD SPORT. This stance is a sort of mix: You will stand sideways on the line, but not square to it, and your shoulders will show a preference of direction. Board sport stance is good for jumping tricks.

LINE MOUNT. A line mount is a good skill to have; it frees you from needing the ground to stand on. It takes you from ground realm to line realm. The line mount has two parts, from hanging on the line to sitting on the line, and from sitting to standing. Both the first and second parts have many variations. Below are a few of each.

Part 1: Hang to Sit Techniques

The **Strong Arm, or Mantle**. This move is a pull-up followed by what climbers call a mantle. Pull then push until you're straight-arming the line in a way that you could gingerly swing around and sit on it.

The **Monkey Bar.** Hanging from your arms, lift or swing your legs up until your head is down and your feet up. Your body should be straight, and you should be hanging from straight arms. Then, bend your legs forward. Their weight will swing your body around, and you'd be in the same position as the mantle, holding your weight on straight arms in front of you. You still need to scoot around to the sitting position. How you position your hands is a matter of practice and preference.

Leg Counter Weight. There is nothing physically hard about this if done correctly. It seems alien to most people, but I've broken it down for you to check out.

Hang to sit
Leg counter weight

Fig. 81. Lift both feet onto left side of line.

Fig. 82. Slide right foot up the line and lift with arms.

Fig. 83. Position very top of left leg on the line.

Fig. 84. Swing feet out, holding body close to line.

Fig. 85. Don't struggle. Feet should counterweight.

Fig. 86. Scoot as close to foot as possible.

*Fig. 87. Foot close.
(One foot seated rest).*

*Fig. 88. Seated with no
counterweight.*

Fig. 89. Hanging your legs below the line provides stability.

PART 2: SIT-TO-STAND

All sit-to-stand mounts are easier if you're facing downhill. If a line is setup level, it is always downhill to the center. Whichever way you do your hang-to-sit technique, it should set you up to be facing downhill.

I think it's more comfortable to sit on the line slightly off to one side of the center. It is important to find a way that is comfortable for you.

Chongo Grab

The first sit-to-stand variation is the Chongo Grab, named after Chuck "Chongo" Tucker. While sitting on the line, place one foot in front of you. With one foot on the line and one foot hanging, this is still a seated rest. Now you need to start balancing. Focused and balanced, you will lift your hanging foot onto the line, then reach down and quickly grab the line in front of you. Pull yourself onto your feet, then let go and try to balance. When Chongo first started flirting with this idea, it looked desperate, but over time he got it to work well.

One Foot on the Line

The next sit-to-stand mount starts at the one-foot seated rest (with one foot on the line and one foot hanging). This mount can be done in a static way, with no dynamic moves, but I will reveal the tricks that make it dynamic and easier. Any line mount can benefit from the bounce of the line, when you're in sync with the bounce. Rocking back as you sit, staying in sync with the bounce also gives you a little extra lift.

Starting at the one-foot seated rest with a very slight bounce, you can rock back, while you lift your foot onto the line. At the top of the bounce, rock forward and stand. With all seated mounts, the closer your feet are to your buttocks, the easier it will be for you to stand.

Two Feet on the Line

It is also possible for you to put both feet on the line, balance on it, lean forward, and stand up. Once you put both feet on the line, all your weight is above it, and you have to balance. This takes some practice, as balancing close to the line is a little different than standing. Sitting completely above the line requires stillness and finesse. I like to sit there and get as still as possible, as balanced as I can, *before* standing.

The closer your feet are to where you sit determines how easy or possible it is to stand from that position. I turn my right foot sideways, with the line crossing my foot at the back of my arch. This allows me to get my foot very close, with my left foot in front of my right. From this position, without bouncing it is possible for you to reach your arms forward, lean forward onto your feet, and stand.

Two feet on the Line
Sit-to-Stand

Fig. 90.
Sit with two
feet on the
line.

Fig. 91.
Lean
forward.

Fig. 92.
Squat.

Fig. 93.
Stand.

Figs. 94-95. Notice how close my feet are together, and how my right foot is turned.

Stand-to-Sit

The opposite of the sit-to-stand technique, stand-to-sit, is a little more difficult. There is no bounce to help. If you can get low enough, you can sit down on the line. If you can't get low enough, you have your choice of the reverse grab or the drop. The drop is about aiming, committing, and hoping for the best.

If you walk to near the end of the line, **turn around and then sit**. You will have the "hill" of the line to your advantage and you may not have to commit to the drop.

Sit-to-stand and stand-to-sit increase with difficulty as you eliminate dynamics and slope advantage.

Under-Over

Under-over encompasses the stand-to-sit technique, and allows you to lie down, roll under, hang-to-sit and sit-to-stand, (sit-to-stand not shown again).

Sit down slowly.

*Slide feet out and
hook with right foot*

Grab line and start balancing
with foot .

Lie down.

Balance with foot.

Slowly go under.

Swing feet around.   *Leg counter weight.*

Squat

The lower you can squat the easier it will be to transition to and from sitting.

Drop knee

No hands

With no hands and arms to wave around, you need to rely on balanced knees, hips and shoulders.

Telemark Cross Train

To get those telemark skiing muscles back in shape, step and bounce at the same time, bending knees deeply while walking. Think snow.

Swing

To swing, push off of one side. I find it useful to only push on one side, and wait for the line to respond. Allow the line to swing in its natural rhythm. Push again, and the line will swing a little more. Be patient; don't push too hard.

Ride the Line

To ride bounce and swing at the same time. This is an advanced technique that requires a narrow line; I prefer nine-sixteenths or eleven-sixteenths tubular webbing for this. Like the swing, push on one side then add a bounce. Let it build slowly and rhythmically.

10.

VISUALIZATION

Visualization is a very useful technique for slackline, at any level of ability. It is just as important for high-line or yard-line. Many athletes use visualization, so many people may be familiar with it, but I will go over the slack-specifics.

For some people visualization seems too much like pretending. It is **not** pretending; rather, it is *imagining.* To imagine is the first step to creating anything, including a skill.

The first time I saw someone slacklining, I had already walked chain and rope, so I knew what that felt like. I watched as the walker wildly swung the line back and forth. I tried to understand how one would master the slackline. To think every move through was to see disaster at every turn. So I focused on trying to understand *what* it felt like. I empathized with the acrobats while I watched them every day for two weeks. During that time and after

I returned home, I spent a lot of time thinking about slackline. Before I fell asleep at night, I remembered what it looked like and imagined what it would feel like to walk and ride with such ease and grace. I imagined I could do it, and I imagined I could really feel balance and grace. When I finally bought a line, I could already walk it.

I suggest that you start to visualize you can easily walk the line, as soon as possible. It is very helpful if you can observe a highly skilled walker. Watch them and visualize *in your body* what the movements feel like. Make sure you are observing a skilled walker. To visualize bad style or limitations can be detrimental to the learning process.

The most important rule of visualization in slacklining is to **never visualize falling**.

It's your imagination. Imagine what you want to happen.

If you are just starting out, you need to know what the slackline feels like underfoot. You need to know what it feels like to be balanced. Once you have been on the slackline for a short time, you will know a little about both.

Sometimes it's hard to visualize not falling when your real life practice sessions are filled with falls. When you start to visualize being on the line, take note of what you see: if you automatically fall in your imagination, you're *expecting* to fall.

Visualization is most effective right before or after sleep. Take some deep breaths, feel balanced, then imagine you ease your weight on to the line. Feel the line press against the bottom of your foot. Step your other foot slowly on to the line. The line swings softly and you dampen its effect by keeping your weight low, pointing your knees toward the side that needs more weight. You feel balanced, centered, and focused in your body.

You don't need to reach way out to regain your balance. You don't need to lose your balance at all. Balance is more about reaching in than reaching out. Remember this while visualizing.

No matter what level you walk at, visualization can help make you better. Visualize as many aspects and details of your surroundings as possible. Most importantly visualize success of the goal. Whether it's to cross the line in your yard, or a still unsent highline, visualizing completion is powerful.

11.
THE ART OF BALANCE

Balance is something;
It exists without you,
And moves through you,
like love.

Balancing and photo by Scott Balcom, 1989.

I HAVE PURSUED an interest in balance for most of my life. I have engaged in balance activities that have nothing to do with slackline, yet the feeling of balance is still the same. I have included different aspects of balance so people can become more aware of its nuances and what balance feels like. It is my belief that once you develop your sense of balance, you can start to identify it in other aspects of life that have nothing to do with gravity.

Balance is key

Here are three types of balance to consider:
  1. Counterweight
  2. Static
  3. Dynamic

Counterweight Balance

Photos on this page by by Phora Craigh, 1992.

Scott Balcom on his unfinished kinetic balance sculpture. This piece balanced a sealed bearing on a steel rod so that it could rotate freely.

In counterweight balance, the center of gravity is below the balance point.

Old style scales and mobiles work on this principle.

A bogus circus trick involves someone riding a bicycle on a high wire with a girl on a trapeze hanging **under** the bicycle. Although the person on the bicycle weighs more than the girl underneath, she is further from the line, which brings the center of gravity below the line. Therefore, no adjustments need to be made and no skill is involved.

That trick should not be confused with the real high-wire bicycle tricks. In the real tricks, there is nothing **under the line** for counter balance.

Making mobiles is an excellent exercise in counterweight balance. The shape of an object has everything to do with how it balances and how it will hang.

The mobile building lesson is two-fold; first you have the act of building something of balance; the second is watching the interaction of balance with movement. A well-designed mobile will not let its components crash in to one another, no matter the combination of movements. The trick to building a mobile is to start at the bottom and work your way up.

Static Balance

Rock garden and photo by Scott Balcom, Tucson Arizona, 1989.

Static balance is like a tenuously balanced rock. Although the rocks sometimes seem as if they're defying gravity, they aren't. Like the saltshaker trick (pictured below), you cannot balance the shaker on its edge, on a smooth, clean table. But a little salt can give you a base even though very small, to center the weight on.

Scott Balcom, 2003.

Stacking rocks can be a great exercise in static balance. When I do this, I do not attempt to balance the rocks by eye, but by feel, empathizing with the plumb-ness of each rock. Precarious balances are beautiful, but very temporary.

Dynamic Balance

In dynamic balance, adjustments need to be made. In the real world, a pyramid cannot balance upside down on its point, and if it could, the slightest breeze or vibration would upset it. Just like driving a car down a straight highway, you'll need to make corrections. Activities like skiing, skating, and surfing employ dynamic balance, because of the need to make corrections and adjustments.

Counterweight and static balance can be mathematically predicted, but dynamic balance cannot be. You could never *predict* the adjustments someone would need to make to cross a slackline. The subtleties and variables are too great. Each time you cross the line, it will be different. That's why dynamic balance is a language of correction, a conversation with the line. Listen for balance.

Gravity

Photo by Mark Arinsberg, 2004.

Gravity pulls straight down on everything. Imagine you can feel this.

Gravity pulls straight down on you. Of course you can feel it. It's everywhere, but how much have you thought about it? How much are you aware of which direction is **straight down**?

ON

I say this aloud at the critical moment,
The moment just before doubt jumps in.
If allowed in, doubt will have its way,
because the moment is so short.
ON

On

Seven frames per second

Like Music

People often like to listen to music while they walk, and walking the line is also a lot like music itself. In music, you need a musician and an instrument, but neither **is** the music. In slackline, you have the line and the walker, but neither is the movement. Just as different musicians can play the same instrument different ways, everyone who gets good at slackline brings a style with them. This style can vary greatly. For example, to walk the line as if it were a drum is to bounce out a rhythm. The centering effect of the bounce lends a certain user-friendly aspect to the drum walk. Although keeping the beat can be a little tricky, turning is the hard part. A drum-walk turn, without missing a beat, should not be attempted by anyone that does not have a solid turn. To walk the line like you're playing lead guitar is to have no plan: a spontaneous expression of line and body. This is one of my favorite things to do.

Slow Time Down

If you could think faster you would have more time to react. Riding the line (swinging and bouncing at the same time) teaches this. When I first started swinging the line, I ended up on the ground so fast, I had no idea what happened. I started paying closer attention to how I ended up on the ground. Slowly, I became aware of the moments between the moments, which gave me more time to react.

Accidents often happen either faster than you can think, or in slow motion. To have more time to react is like the slow motion fall, but instead of just witnessing the event, you have time to react. I imagine hitting a fastball or being quick in martial arts requires a similar ability to "slow time down".

Personal Energy

Personal energy is something some people think about only in terms of quantity: "I have no energy" or "I have a lot of energy." In our analytic society, this seems to be the only measurement we are willing to place on our personal energy. The whole life force that animates the body has been reduced to this single measurement based on the experience of what is normal and whether the present state is more or less than that norm.

Some people have a better understanding of energy. The martial arts traditions are evidence of this greater understanding of personal energy/life force. Cultivating an awareness of your energy and connection with your life force, then focusing and directing that energy will greatly enhance your slacklining.

Bring Up Your Energy

I met a man who was taking horseback riding lessons from an old, strong, and silent horseman—the kind of guy who understands horses better than people. His way was very Zen. Always firm but never cruel, the trainer would say, "bring up your energy," when he thought the student was letting the horse take the lead. The idea, it would seem, is to be in control, but to make as subtle a gesture as possible. You don't kick the horse when you want to go; you simply "bring up your energy." This story reminded me of slackline. The subtleness of the gestures and the way focusing the energy of your intent is the best way to stay in control and confident.

A narrow mind is like a long corridor that only leads to one place.

An Exercise of Perception

Traditional western linear thinking seeks order through logic. Slackline is neither orderly nor logical. Imagine perception as a muscle that always performs the same task. It would be hard at first to use that muscle in a different way. What follows is an exercise in perception. This is not a test of truth, but a lens to view the same old thing in a different way.

The Shortest Distance Between Two Points

People often quote the geometric truth, "the shortest distance between two points is a straight line," as if it has some bearing on our everyday lives, as if it were a guiding principle or rule of thumb. For over twenty years I have sought straight lines. My life as a carpenter has been a persistent pursuit of perpendicular perfection. I developed my eye the way a musician develops an ear. To see straight and square. Through this pursuit, I came to believe that truly straight lines over distance probably don't exist outside of the imagination. The straightest line I can think of is the ocean to sky interface on a very clear day, even though the ocean curves and undulates. Sure, there are lots of straight-ish lines around and lots of small objects that are arguably straight, but these are mostly man made. In the natural world, there are very few things that would qualify as straight.

One day while walking the line, I had an insight: what if the slackline is a better model than the straight line. Slackline is that ideal, very nearly straight line, right up until you step on it. That ideal perfect line is changed by your presence. Not only is the path you walk no longer straight, the path itself is changed. What if this way of seeing were closer to the true nature of lines and the true nature of life?

You cannot walk the line without changing it; you cannot walk through life without changing it. **Your presence matters.**

In the real world, it is hard to travel in a straight line. For example, while driving down a straight road (as mentioned before) you still need to steer eventually. In those magic moments in which you appear to be driving in a straight line without steering, some might argue you are traveling in a straight line. I would counter that the wheels of your vehicle are going round and round and are not traveling in a straight line. If you painted a spot on the edge of your tire and drove down the street, the spot's path would be closer to that of a bouncing ball than a straight line.

Air bubbles rising through water may rise straight briefly, but then they start bobbing back and forth in a path reminiscent of a skier or snowboarder. I have heard that slow motion films of rain falling reveal that raindrops move in much the same way.

Light can travel straight, but light travels in *waves*.

Our present paradigm places a premium on perpendicular that precludes any other possibility, this is potentially problematic.

SEEK BALANCE

12. HIGHLINE

It is not the focus of this book to teach highline,
nor is highlining the ultimate expression of slackline.

Photo by Kate Balcom, 1985.

*Scott Balcom on the first slackline crossing of The Lost Arrow Spire, July 13,
1985.*

AWHILE BACK, a climbing magazine had an article about climbers
in Yosemite Valley and what they did while not climbing. On one
page was a picture of Dean Potter walking a highline, while on the
facing page was a picture of Dan Osmon rope jumping hundreds of

feet off a cliff. The next month, a reader had written to say how close to death Potter had been while walking this highline. He went on to say how his "back of a napkin" calculations had Potter's life a few nylon fibers away from ending. The harsh irony of this is that it was Dan Osmon, not Dean Potter who died doing a 900-foot rope jump right about that same time. Dan Osman's death was a surprise. Many believed him to be a master rigger who knew what he was doing.

Engineers shudder at the thought of highline, because of the directions of force involved. I have not taken engineering classes and have not done the math, but I have walked on bootlace. It did break under normal slackline use and it didn't take very long, once we got it tight enough. I have spent many hours body weight testing one inch and nine-sixteenths inch tubular nylon.

Up until recently, I could remember seeing only one piece of nine-sixteenths break. But I have now seen people who walk a tighter style than me break lines. It is important to have a lot of experience to draw from in assessing if you are within working strength of a given setup.

It's your life; treat it with respect.

When I have walked high, **I have had two pieces of nine-sixteenths inside a piece of one inch tubular for a stronger line**. Other highliners use three pieces of one inch that they tighten individually at different tensions, one line tight, one medium and one loose. Then they tyrolean across and tape the lines together with climbing tape. Taped lines are more adjustable and generally stronger than threaded lines.

A regular yard setup should never be used up high.

The fact is, I cannot tell you that highline is safe. You need to do your own testing close to the ground, and lots of it.

Every highline setup is unique, so it is hard to give good instruction. Here are some rules that are helpful:

- Always protect the lines from rubbing against rock, concrete or any thing else the line might come in contact with.
- Triple everything.
- Equalize all anchors.
- Only use high quality webbing, and know its strengths and limitations.
- Use no less than two leashes with two locking carabiners, or solid rings. If carabiners are used, always wrap tape around the gate to cover any sharp edges.
- Never trust your life to any sort of tightening device: **always back it up**.
- Find out the proper way to set rock anchors.
- Know how to use all your equipment.
- **Anything you try up high should have been tried on the ground first, <u>many times</u>.**
- **Never tighten the line more than you do on the ground.**
- Always remember that a system is only as strong as its weakest link.
- Avoid using a clove hitch, it's a very weak knot.

Those who push the limits… will eventually find them.

For more information on highline, see *Walking Over Air, The Art Of Highlining* by Chongo.

14.
A SLACKLINE STORY

DURING THE SUMMER of 1983, while in Yosemite Valley, I saw these two guys walking on webbing. They could bounce on the line and wildly swing it back and forth. They could do all kinds of tricks, but the one that intrigued me the most was riding the line (bouncing and swinging at the same time to make the line move in a sort of circle or ellipse). When others tried to walk on their line, it looked very precarious. The line would shake, even with a spotter. When the spotter let go, few could stay on the line, and at that point it looked rather dangerous. I tried it, and it felt dangerous to me too.

I was already experimenting with walking on chain, cable, and different ropes, but something was lacking. I could only turn a couple of times, but these guys could fly. I had once considered webbing but thought it too squirrelly. Here was Adam Grosowsky and Jeff Ellington with a command over that squirrelly-ness that made it look like a dance.

I watched them everyday and I imagined what it felt like to ride the line. At the bottom of the circle, it's like being at the bottom of a swing: you're pushing positive G force, but when you go across the top, you're floating nearly weightlessly. The point at which you go from near weightlessness to positive G force was the part that concerned me most. This is like holding a rubber band away from your face with your feet, balancing while increasing tension. Not to mention that this whole dynamic process happens quickly, maybe one cycle per second.

Adam and Jeff had a plan to walk the gap between the Lost Arrow Spire and the rim of the valley just below Yosemite Point. On the same wall as Yosemite falls, the Lost Arrow Spire is an incredible monolithic finger with great exposure, the same gap as the classic Yosemite Tyrolean traverse poster and post card.

The top of the spire (as close as I can determine through studying a topo map) is just about 2890 feet above the valley floor.

When I heard their intentions my inner voice said, "I'm supposed to do that." That little intuitive outburst surprised me, and I thought, "What are you talking about? You don't have the skill or the nerve." Adam and Jeff had a steel cable for the spire walk, and a second for a practice line that they had left set up in the forest. Rangers confiscated the practice cable.

They practiced on nylon, and then went up to the spire. It was late afternoon and I was in the lodge parking lot. This girl who had been hanging out with Adam and Jeff came around and said she had seen them walk the Lost Arrow Spire. A group of us positioned ourselves at a spot to see the spire, but we couldn't really see anything. The next day Adam and Jeff returned. I went to congratulate them and they informed me that they had been unsuccessful in their quest. Their friend must have seen them do the tyrolian, and thought they were walking. Occasionally a rumor resurfaces that Adam and Jeff walked the Lost Arrow Spire that summer, in 1983. I'm sure the false eyewitness is responsible for this. I spoke with Jeff years later and he said he had not been back.

According to Adam and Jeff's account, it seemed to me that their downfall was practicing on nylon, then attempting the spire on cable. Modern tightropers use cable, but guy it off as much as possible and use a balance pole. The vibration of an unguyed tight cable, runs the length of the line then bounces off the end and comes back at you. At that moment, it is nearly impossible to stay on the cable. The weight of the cable makes the feedback very strong and always seems to be reverberating opposite of what you're dealing with at the time.

I went home and thought about slackline for about a month before I got around to getting a line. During that time, I still imagined what it felt like to walk and ride the line. When I finally got a line and set it up, I could walk it.

Photo by Scott Balcom.

Chris Carpenter riding the line, 1983.
Chris had been on the Yosemite trip with me, and we practiced together and pushed each other and both excelled quickly at this time.

Photo by Chris Carpenter.

Scott Balcom on a 117' line, 1984.

Once I felt confidant on one-inch I started experimenting with different lines until I had walked every line the local climbing store carried.

At this time, I was looking for the answer to the questions, "What line is strong enough to walk up high with? What line would I trust my life with?" The lesson I had drawn from Adam and Jeff was practice on the same type of line that you expect to walk up high with. I decided a break from tradition was necessary and that nylon webbing needed to be used up high. I went out and bought an eighty-five-foot piece of two-inch tubular nylon.

Around Thanksgiving 1983 Chris and I tried our first high walk. At a large bridge with twelve huge cement arches in Pasadena, California, Chris and I strung a line from a column at the top of one arch to the corresponding column on the next arch. Big wall master Rob Slater had come up from San Diego for the weekend, and although he could barely walk the line on the ground, his go-for-it spirit was a great help. After climbing the arches and stringing the line, no one really had the nerve to step off. Luckily, it was getting dark, so we left the line fixed and headed back to my house.

That night, Rob swore that when we went back in the morning he would step off. The next morning, Rob was focused and determined. He clipped his leashes to the line, got in position, and, true to his word, stepped off.

For a short moment, Rob stood on the line above the void. But lacking the skill to continue, he fell, catching himself with both hands.

We set up an overhead hand line to hold onto while each of us walked across from arch to arch. Chris walked to the middle of the span and let go of the hand line.

Photo by Scott Balcom.

Rob Slater takes the dive while Chris Carpenter looks on.

It sprang out of his reach and he walked to the lines end. I tried this. It was scary at first, then I cautiously walked off the line and stepped onto the arch. Chris was up again. He stepped out and then fell. Now it was my turn again. I took two quick steps and tried to recover. At first it felt very scary, and I was unsure. One of the hard parts of stepping onto a highline is the way you must assess the line very quickly. I kept my balance, and then I had this locked-in feeling where I knew I wouldn't fall. I walked to the end of the line. Chris made a successful crossing, and we both walked a few more times after that.

Of course, there have been many tightrope walks over the years, but as far as I know this was the first high slackline walk.

We set up my two-inch line in the park at eighty feet. When we got the line tight enough, I saw the flutter. In the slightest breeze, the line fluttered back and forth across its width. As the flutter builds, the line also starts moving up and down, a lot. This would never do at the Lost Arrow Spire. The breeze we had in the park was only about five miles an hour. We found that a fluttering line can be walked, only with greater effort. The longest part of the line will flutter the most. As you walk into the flutter, it cancels out, but then starts up behind you.

On the bridge, we used a belay, so we didn't really trust our lives to a single piece of two-inch tubular. Two-inch is strong stuff, but when you're betting the whole show, and there is no shortage of people telling you that what you're doing is foolish, you want to be sure.

Photo by Chris Carpenter.

Scott Balcom on the first high slackline walk, November 1983.

I decided multiple lines were necessary. I was familiar with electricians pulling wire through conduit with fish-tapes. I looked at the inside of a piece of one-inch tubular and thought two pieces of nine-sixteenths would be loose. I bought two pieces of three-mil perlon and two pieces of nine-sixteenths tubular to go inside of a piece of one-inch tubular, all seventy-five feet long.

The idea was to put the two nine-sixteenths, one atop the other, with the two pieces of three-mil on either side and pull them *through* the piece of one-inch. As it turned out, all the lines did not fit inside the one-inch. I eliminated one of the pieces of three-mil.

Then, I fashioned a clothes hanger into a tool that I could thread both pieces of nine-sixteenths, one atop the other, and the piece of three-mil next to that inside the one-inch. I fished the clothes hanger into the one-inch and pulled the other lines inside. Chris helped by holding on to the one inch.

In this way, we made a triple line (plus the three-mil perlon). This "tripler" is a heavy line. The heaviness of a line adds to the feedback and requires greater tightening capacity.

Adam and Jeff had said the spire walk was around sixty-two feet. The bridge walk was short, maybe twenty feet. Chris and I walked the bridge with the triple line at least once, and in the park we found two trees sixty-two feet apart to walk between. (As it turned out, the spire walk is closer to fifty-five feet).

In the summer of '84, Chris Carpenter and I went to Yosemite Valley with the intention of walking from the Lost Arrow Spire to the rim of the valley. I persuaded Darrin Carter and Bob "the Aidman" to climb the spire for us. We left the valley early in the morning and walked up the Yosemite Falls Trail and up the rim to the spire (four miles and almost 3000 vertical feet). Darrin and Bob walked to the tree at the edge of the rim, tied two ropes end to end (tying one end to the tree), and repelled 250 feet to the notch, then climbed the spire. I set anchors at the flake and waited. Once they got to the top, we set up a tyrolean traverse and I crossed the gap to finish rigging my line. By the time the line was rigged, tightened, and ready to go, it was well past midday.

After almost a year of planning and mental preparation, the moment I had been waiting for had arrived. There I was, standing on top of Lost Arrow Spire, staring at the one-inch line I was to walk. I felt sick. During all my psych training, I thought that all I would have to do is take the first two steps, then I'd be "locked in." (At least that's the way it had been at the Arches, our name for the bridge walk). Sick with fear at the thought of walking **or** doing the tyrolean again. I figured that walking was my only way out. I thought to myself: *It's not **that** far, I walk line all the time. The first step is the crux, and I have not come all this way to chicken out now.*

I stepped on the line and it slid about a foot down the sloping edge of the spire. Rock rarely has a shape perfect for slackline. I wrapped some extra nylon around the line to protect it from the rock and had Bob hold the line in the already slid position with his foot. Chris stayed back on the rim as photographer with the intention of trading places with me after I tried. Darrin stayed on the spire, also with camera in hand. I stepped one foot out on the line; I could feel the vibration of a stiff breeze passing by it. In my altered state of fear, the vibration of the line bothered me, it felt like it was buzzing dangerously, like a power line. I stared at the wall on the other side of the void and tried **not** to look at the valley nearly 3000 feet below. Half a dozen spectators had gathered on the rim and I yelled "come on, cheer me on." I needed the encouragement. Darrin said, "Go, Scott, go." The spectators just got their cameras ready, waiting for some action. The breeze was steady, but I could no longer wait.

With one foot on the line and one foot on the spire, I stepped off. Lonely naked fear is the only way to describe the feeling I had. The exposure is horrendous. I leaned too hard to one side and then the other. I couldn't get it together, and my feet peeled from the line.

On the way down, my right side slid and bounced off the line and I made a one-handed catch. Falling didn't help my psyche any. On the next try, I lost my balance and dove back to the spire. Bob grabbed my arm tightly, but I had it. I got back on the spire and tried to relax. I took some deep breaths, but I started feeling light headed. With another fall, I yelled with frustration and jumped back onto the spire. I was mad now, mad that I hadn't made it the first time. I tried to clear my mind.

I thought of the sequence of events that had led up to this moment. I thought of all the nights, before sleep, when I would visualize stepping off. I imagined that moment a thousand times, accompanied by a surge of adrenalin. In the beginning, I would shake at the thought, but as the months passed, I got used to the idea, until I could sit calmly and think out every detail.

Now all those times came together in that one moment, but my imagination had not been able to conjure the scene before me, nor the psychological impact. My conscious mind was determined, but my discomfort with fear was greater than the feeling of "butterflies" that had been scared to death and lay rotting in my stomach. I could feel the cells of my body individually and in unison screaming "NO, DON'T DO IT!"

I believed the spark of life that animates me will never die. The cells of my body were harder to convince. I could feel them saying, "Maybe you don't die, but we cells do."

Encouragingly, Bob said, "I think you're afraid of the middle of the line." ("Thanks Bob"). This was just one more seed of doubt in my fertile fearful mind.

The no-hands thing never bothered me on the ground, but I so badly wanted something to hold on to. I had been taking the first two steps, but there was no locked-in feeling. In fact, the feeling was more like a psychologically painful tearing away, as if the slight electro-magnetic field that surrounds me needs to ground to something solid.

I'm not sure how many times I backed off or fell, or how long I sat there, waiting for the mood to change or the breeze to die down. I decided that I had been giving up too easily. I psyched-up for another attempt. Taking two quick steps, I stepped out from the spire and tried hard to balance. I was so determined to stay out there that by the time I realized I was falling it was too late. I fell to my left away from the line. I looked for the line to grab onto and saw that my feet were still on it, well behind the direction my hands were heading. I looked in front of me. I was falling into the throat of the Lost Arrow chimney, framed by my outstretched arms. In that moment, I couldn't help but remember a story I had read about an early climbing exploration in which a guy repelled off the end of his rope into the Lost Arrow chimney. I wondered if I was its next meal.

I saw the notch between the spire and the wall a mere 250 feet below, and then I saw the valley floor, stretched out roughly 2885 feet 6 1/2 inches below my outstretched arms. My leashes were tied to my right side and had swung me around. As the swing ended, I jumped back onto the spire, like a cat out of a bath. I had never been so scared in all my life as I was falling into the Lost Arrow chimney.

Darrin said, "You looked like superman with your arms out in front of you, flying through the sky. You screamed like a girl."

I tried again. I stepped out, then turned back. If I turned right, I could jump back at the spire and stand on a little lip about five feet below the line. If I went left and didn't make the top of the spire, there was nothing to stand on. I spun left and dove at the rock, one hand firmly palming the top of the spire. My feet had nowhere to go, and I bounced off the rock and took another dangling panorama, this time framed by my feet. The "other side" was psychologically too far away. I was done, and it was getting too late for Chris to try. We packed up our stuff and hiked down the trail.

I see now that my training had been inadequate in at least three ways. First, I like to look at the ground in front of me while the line moves past it. At the spire, I looked at the wall past the line, but it's far below. It's hard to tell how large the strips are on the wall. My perspective was all messed up. second, I thought I would get this great "locked-in" feeling after a few steps, and that never happened. In my visualization, I stepped one foot out on the line. The day was beautiful, the breeze slight and the air sweet. I imagined I would take two steps out and would feel locked-in. I didn't routinely visualize stepping onto the ledge at the **end** of the walk and the elation I'd feel. The third flaw was in the psych training itself. It wasn't scary enough. There was a strange comfort in having a roof overhead at the bridge, or maybe the bridge wasn't high enough or long enough. Whatever it was, the bridge wasn't scary enough to prepare me for the spire.

Fresh from my most recent failure, I was changed. My comfort level had been blown out of the water. Things that used to intimidate me no longer did. The most intense aspect of this effect wore off after a few months and I was not sure if the effect would last a whole year, when I would try again.

In the summer of 1985, I went to Yosemite Valley with one goal: to walk the line. Chris, who had just graduated high school and was moving to San Diego to get ready for College, opted out.

During that year, my training was not about walking but primarily about visualization. I did not know how many steps it would take to cross or exactly how long it would take to get there. Instead, I focused on the part that had eluded me the year before: stepping onto the ledge at the other end of the line. I imagined that I would step on that rock, feeling the rush of elation and triumph.

I had no climbing goals that summer, though I planned to spend several weeks in the valley. Every day I'd look up at the spire and imagine I could see myself walking the void between. The truth is, it is so high that it's hard to see people up there in the middle of the day.

I had a pair of slackline shoes that had a checkered design on them. I had drawn symbols and designs on all the light colored squares. Shoes that are good for slackline are not good for hiking, since they have no support and smooth soles, but as part of my psych training I wore those shoes everywhere that summer. Every time I looked down at my feet, I was reminded to focus. The thinness of the soles made me aware of everything I stepped on. The lack of traction on steep dusty trails made me conscious and deliberate with every step I took.

I started spending time with a young woman who'd just graduated from college and was working at the park for the summer. Her name was Kate. She was lovely.

My dad had told me to let him know when I was going to do the walk. If I could commit to a date, he would rent a video camera and drive up from Southern California to shoot the event. Back then, few people owned video cameras, and the cameras and batteries were big and heavy. My dad, who is not much of a camper, said he would pack all the camera equipment up the trail, spend the night, and shoot the event in the morning. I still needed someone to climb the spire for me. About then, I ran in to Matt Dancy, someone I'd climbed with in previous summers. He and his partner, Ken Klis, agreed to help.

For my attempt the year before, I thought we would have to carry too much gear if we spent the night. I hadn't factored the wind that comes up every afternoon, as the wall below heats up. This time I wanted to *be* set up in the morning to catch it while it was calm.

Scott Balcom at dress rehearsal,
July 11, 1985

Photo by Raleigh Winter.

A guy named Paul Borne had started walking line two weeks before. He had successfully crossed the line on the ground only a few times but thought he'd like to give the spire a shot.

I hiked the falls trail with my dad, Kate, and my sister Raleigh. By the time we reached the spire, Matt and Ken had already climbed it.

Paul and I geared up. Paul took one end of the line and repelled down the fixed rope to the top of the spire. I repelled with the other end of the line down to the flake and set the anchors. Once the line was rigged, we climbed the ropes back up to the rim. Paul waited for that moment to learn how to operate rope ascenders but made the rim before total dark.

I had only known Kate for a month, but we already had a bond. I told her not to be scared for me, and that I could do this.

July 13, 1985

The wind had been blowing out of the high country all night. The next morning, it started to calm. When it was still, my dad said, "You'd better get out there, Scott."

The year before, I couldn't believe how scary it was. I was dreading the possibility of an equally horrifying time.

Paul and I rappelled out to the spire and tightened the line. I was tense, but not as bad as the year before. After a few attempts, I felt better, not worse. I tried many times, and once I got almost halfway across, and **then** I fell. I was mad, not scared. I'd been way out there, past the hard part. I didn't feel that psychologically painful tearing away but more of a feeling of jumping into cold water. I went back to the spire hand over hand, not bothering to throw my feet up on the line. Another time, I walked nearly a third the way out, but most of my falls were in the first three steps. The other side started to feel far away; I could feel myself lusting after it, wanting to *be* on the other side.

One adjustment that I made for the visual perception problem I'd had the year before was to hang a backpack under the line by one of the fixed ropes. This allowed me to see how much the slackline moved in relation to the rope. I also asked Ken to rappel down to the flake, so I would have a human reference. I stood there staring at him at the end of the line. Calling to him, "It's not *that* far." "No, it's not," he agreed.

I tried again, walking four or five steps, and then I started to lose my balance. I thought about how I had been out this far only a few times before and that I needed to focus on my balance more. Consciously and deliberately, I focused only on the balance of the moment. I avoided falling and took another step. I stayed focused and thought only about the correction of the moment. Soon, I was in the middle of the line. Many people were watching, but no one said a word. I could hear only camera shutters up on the rim. I was blind to the exposure, only seeing Ken on the other side with an out stretched hand. I finally got that locked-in feeling in the last twenty feet. Still, no one said a word.

The last few steps were effortless. I stepped onto the flake. It felt great, and everyone cheered. My friend Tony, who had walked up the trail that morning, called out, "You might as well jump now. It doesn't get any better!"

It was a very good summer. I walked the spire *and* got the girl.

What Did You Learn?

The next day, back in the valley, my dad interviewed me on video-tape. He asked me what I'd learned. I knew that I had wanted to conquer my own fear and not the spire, but I was unsure about the final lesson. A few months later, it hit me. I had been unable to get to the other side while lusting after it, *wishing* I were already there. Only when I focused all my energy on where I was at the moment, my corrections of the moment, was I able to reach the other side. This was the ultimate "be here now" lesson, but I'd never grasped the gravity of **the moment**, not this week, or today or even this minute, but the very moment between the future and the past, the only moment there is.

About The Author

Scott Balcom began slacklining with friends in 1983 in his hometown of South Pasadena, California. In November 1983, he and his friend Chris Carpenter walked what is believed to be the first high slackline ever. Scott Balcom was the first person to walk a slackline between the Lost Arrow Spire and the rim of Yosemite Valley at 2,890 feet above the valley floor in Yosemite National Park on July 13, 1985. Scott has been a carpenter since age eighteen, at one time specializing in straw bale construction in Tucson, Arizona. He has always had an interest in balance and has explored many avenues to further his understanding through sculpture, rock gardens and slacklining. Scott is an innovator in the slackline world and has recently been inventing tools to make slackline more accessible to others. He currently lives in Ashland, Oregon, with his wife and son. For more information visit **www.slackline.net**, or **www.slackdaddytools.com**.